The Inspired Advocate:

8 Attributes Every Advocate Must Embrace

Rhonda Thomas-Hicks

Foreword

S peaking up for yourself or others is the first step of advocacy. But, what next? This is such a refreshing book to read. It is the GPS on navigating through the heartbreaks, disappointments and setbacks just trying to be heard.

I served on my local school board for ten years, and I frequently encountered parents that felt helpless and hopeless when dealing with the educational institution (particularly if there was a disagreement with an assessment made regarding their student). The underlying question for them was, "How do I make myself heard in a field of purported experts? What is the next step when the expert findings should be overruled?"

If there is one hope that is uppermost on my wish list for those parents who find themselves in a conflicting situation, it is developing strategies to assist them in finding their voice. This is the most frightening step because the only thing a parent is armed with is the belief in his/her student that is unsupported by predictive data experts frequently rely on for a student's educational plan. The crucial step structuring a personalized plan of action to ensure expectations are met is equally daunting.

It is common to think that the educational institution (*or any institution for that matter*) has the best interest of your student at heart. Nevertheless, what happens when you discover fault to this and realize the hope or assumption is incorrect? Worthy of note is "the exception to every rule". So, how does one go about getting a seat at the table? We relinquish control often to 'authority'. Wherein lies the question, "whose authority should reign over the success of my student or loved one?"

I love this book, and anyone that has ever doubted themselves or their ability to advocate should read it!

Betty Arnold, USD 259 Wichita Public Schools Board of Education from July 2007 - January 2017. She served as School Board President from 2011 - 2012 and VP from 2010 - 2011, 2015 - 2016 and 2017 - 2018.

Acknowledgements

Without the divine inspiration from the Lord, it would have been impossible for me to advocate for my children. I acknowledge God for carrying me through the disappointments along this journey that I share with you. I live and move in God. I cannot get away from him.

Next, my dear mother, Hazel Charlene Hopson Thomas, my best friend, my confidant, my love who departed for her heavenly home October 13, 2018 was my biggest supporter. The power of my mom's love and wisdom exudes throughout every part of me. Such an impact mom had on me! Advocacy started with her. She let nothing stop her from advocating and checking on my brother and me. My mother taught me how to stand up for what I believe in even if I am the only one standing. My rock. I truly miss you mama.

Kamika and Kevin Jr., whom I lovingly call Mika and Perez, never knew about their learning problems because I did not share that with them. I simply shared solutions and equipped them with what they needed to excel academically. Mika and Perez, I wrote this book so you will see in writing the steps and measures I took to map out a successful academic career for you. I love you two so much.

Many educators, friends, family and colleagues supported me - too many names to list here. You know who you are, and I salute you and thank you. I thank Cindy Sharp, my editor. She made me feel empowered as she assisted me in conveying a simple yet impactful story to you. Lastly, I thank Betty Arnold for writing The Foreword. I am honored.

Finally, I acknowledge every person who reads this book and takes action advocating for what he/she believes!

Contents

Preface

An organization that was providing services to my son asked me to present a parent's testimony to the school board. I gladly replied, "Yes"! When I began my testimonial speech, I offered this quote:

"Our lives begin to end the day we become silent about things that matter." Martin Luther King Jr.

These events were the catalysts that awoke the 'inspired advocate' within me.

Initially, I was exhausted on most days, but this particular day I became overwhelmed. The stress was both physical and mental because my job was unusually demanding, bills were past due and I was living paycheck to paycheck. Finally, I stopped a moment to rest, regroup by spending time with my three-year-old daughter and noticed she was not communicating nor understanding me properly for her age. Yet another frustration of extreme importance added to my heavy stack of duties.

After that day, I began to search high and low looking for any information that could help me with my child's learning problems.

I sought everywhere and everyone, but people denied any advice, help or resources. Many of the programs gave discounts for counseling, self-help books, tutoring, evaluations and other assistance, but I did not qualify for any because my income was too high. The federal and state-funded programs that offered support were designed for low-income households. I was just seeking assistance of some kind; however, there was nothing for median incomes.

Passionately, I have always known that education is the passport to success. Quality education is to be valued, and I felt threatened by this obstacle facing my daughter and me. After months of searching, I received a good lead about a program that could serve my daughter with reading and speech therapy services. I called them excitedly and thought, "Finally, this is it!"

When the representative answered the phone, I asked her to set up an appointment, but she quickly interrupted and inquired instead about my income. At first, I hung up because I assumed it would not end in my favor. After contemplating awhile on the fact that I did not make enough to get the services by myself, I called her back with my income. She point blankly and without hesitancy or compassion responded 'no'!

In the intervening time, my health insurance provided coverage for a limited amount of speech therapy sessions for my daughter. I had to come up with the remaining costs myself which was not only expensive but distressing as well.

Nevertheless, I called several other programs that I thought would aid my daughter. But even with my income tax report, the answer was the only way I would qualify for the program was to quit my job and get on welfare! Several agencies simply and rudely hung up on me without the courtesy of a proper goodbye!

Keep in mind; I was diligently seeking assistance in my entire city to find answers to my daughter's needs. I was discouraged and felt inadequate and insecure! Clearly, I was totally out of my element being a parent with a desperate cry for help with her child.

Persistence pays off every time and finally an administrator said, "Once your daughter turns five years of age and is attending kindergarten in an educational setting, you can go to her assigned base school and request an assessment." My daughter's speech therapist said as well, "When you have a child with a learning disability, the school district will provide a free assessment. Based off your address just locate her assigned base school and request an assessment."

After having run into so many walls and being very discouraged, I followed through with this pertinent information. The school principal explained the process used which would begin with an IEP (Individual Education Plan). This plan involves the teamwork and expertise of a teacher, speech therapist, psychologist, nurse and a social worker. They would administer a series of tests to assess the educational needs and tools that my daughter needed to overcome her speech and fact retaining-learning issues.

Each specialist gave his or her assessment of my daughter and bleakly relayed to me that she would never read on grade level and would remain two grade levels behind other students. Moreover, with all this information, they still did not offer a solution.

Disappointed, I held my daughter's assessment and sat in my car feeling as if someone kicked me in my stomach. I literally could not breathe. Feeling helpless and not knowing what to do, I thought about how difficult it would be sending my daughter to school knowing she was already 'labeled' to fail? That is how devastating the report sounded to me! I tried to convince myself that now was the time to give up.

As I sat in my car, I began to weep uncontrollably, releasing all of the pinned-up emotions that plagued me for the last year and thinking I had no options. However, that was when I heard a still, quiet voice say within me, "How do they know what she is going to do?" I immediately sat up straight and wiped my eyes. As immediately as I heard that voice, I became empowered with an understanding of what the voice was saying to me.

First, I knew it was the Lord's voice. Secondly, I knew that He was telling me that He had plans for my daughter, so I should consult the One who had created her! Instantly, a pleasant feeling came over me, and my tears stopped. This good feeling felt like a heavy weight lifting off my shoulders. Joy and an extraordinary energy engulfed me. It was a phenomenal moment. I did not know what to do or how to do it but knew God would equip me to handle this task.

The journey was challenging, but I met it 'head-on'! I purchased books, tapes, cds and DVDs then developed a very structured life for my daughter. Every night we read and tackled vocabulary and math through flashcards making sure that homework was completed. I practically lived in the schools! Although I was diligent in my approach, I ran into some educators who had low expectations for her. A few who thought I was too stern, too high-strung and too outspoken labeled me as a "helicopter parent" because I hovered over my daughter pushing her too hard.

Sure, they may have been right, but it did not deter me. I had to follow 'that voice', and I had to be 'a voice' for my daughter who could not retell a story. Until she reached third grade, I never knew about her day. I accepted the word from her teachers and from other students. I knew that some of their reports were not accurate because they would tell me she had a great day, but I would pick her up from school, and she would be in tears!

It was a very scary time for me to say the least. Nevertheless, throughout this process I was divinely empowered with certain attributes that kept me strong, effective and successful. Whenever I was told that my daughter would never do something, I placed that on my 'to do believing list' knowing she would eventually do it!

They said that my daughter would never read on her grade level, but by the end of her first semester of fourth grade, she was reading. For five long years, I asked my daughter daily to relay her day in chronological order, which she could not do.

The progress was slow often, and I got discouraged. Thankfully, I gradually began to see improvement along the way. By the time my daughter reached the eighth grade and enrolled in Algebra, I began to see the fruits of our labor come to completion! I knew the road we were on was the road to academic success! Her academic and social achievements realized in middle school, and I was so grateful.

This success continued as my daughter went on to obtain her high school diploma! Proud moments came to our family when she was able to enroll in Calculus her senior year. She won a highly- acclaimed visual arts award presented to her during her graduation ceremony. Can you imagine how I felt? I am sitting in the audience watching my daughter being recognized and graduating from high school. I was so grateful that I put in the hard work along with my mom, family and many educators. I felt so blessed.

Watching my daughter walk across the stage with friends who experienced our struggle was one of the most joyful days in my life! I felt blessings of true joy flow over my mind and heart remembering with gratefulness the effort I put in on her behalf.

Now my son, who is 6 years younger than his sister, has the same type of learning issues and more. Because of my experience with my daughter, I quickly knew what to do and immediately signed him up with the best school for children with learning disabilities.

Before he entered kindergarten, I met with a well-known physician who assesses children with certain learning disabilities. She did not give my son a good report. I asked her if she would believe me if I introduced her to a person who had the same issues but went on to excel academically. She answered that she would find it hard to believe. I introduced her to my daughter, and we left the meeting. I refused to engage with anyone who did not believe my son could win academically.

There is a purpose for experts, and I visit and communicate with experts on a daily basis. However, as a parent I could not agree with any negative diagnosis for my children without first trying my best to meet and exceed any challenges regarding them. I have done this over the years with both of my children and am so relieved I did.

This time around, the doctor's words about my son did not discourage me because I had already been through the battle with my daughter. My demeanor was very and solidly confident. With gladness I was divinely empowered to advocate for my children which has allowed me to mentor and coach other youth and adults as well.

My son did have the best Kindergarten teacher in the world though. The way she would report my son's progress to me was encouraging. One time, he received a 30% on a test, but the next time he took the same test, he received a 59%. Instead of reporting to me that he failed both tests, she told me that he was improving rapidly! What a great teacher!

Further, I will now discuss the attributes I was equipped with to be able to collaborate with teachers, speech therapists, social workers, psychologists, principals, IEP managers, occupational therapists, school nurses and medical doctors who had a direct and indirect effect on my children and me.

These are attributes every advocate must possess in order to stay the course with their child, student or client. They empower and inspire the advocate to awaken greatness within those whom they are serving.

CHAPTER 1:

BELIEVE

When faced with the idea that my child may never read on grade level or achieve academic success, I was devastated! I was not supposed to be the person to receive such news because I was under the impression that by default, my daughter and son would learn as other children their age, and all would be well. It never crossed my mind that my own children may have a learning disability. Moreover, for whatever reason I was unable to "receive" those words and was in disbelief. Belief would have been easier if I had been knowledgeable in this area, but since I was clueless, it turned into discouragement.

After the IEP meeting, I was distraught because I really had no idea what to do. As I stated, I went to my car and cried and in the midst of that cry, I heard the Lord ask me, "How do they know what she can and cannot do?"

This was all I needed to hear. I understood the question and understood what to do then. I had to believe in myself and that

I would be equipped with the right strategies to turn this bleak outlook of my four-year-old daughter into a victorious one. Remember, I had no clue what to do, but I KNEW WHAT I BELIEVED.

Believe and you shall receive. Early on, I created a definition that would fit throughout this time: *"I must believe in myself without a doubt in my mind that I will be able to perform what is needed and necessary to assist my daughter to academic success!"*

Not only was I able to believe in myself, but I was able to believe in my daughter. Then later on, I was able to believe in my son, every teacher, speech therapist, social worker, nurse and every person who believed and had an impact on both my children. More importantly, I was able to look at my daughter's bleak individual education plan and believe she would defy the odds.

People often ask me if my daughter believed in what I was doing and how she felt as she went through this process. Well, I never made her aware of the learning disability diagnosis, so she did not know the jeopardy she was in academically. It was up to me, the parent/advocate, to recognize and fix the problem.

CHAPTER 2:

Faith

The type of faith I needed was the sort that did not rely on logical proof or material evidence such as test IQ scores. I required the faith that relies on information of what I 'hoped' to see. Visualization is key. I visualized what I wanted to see in my daughter's academic career.

The following three steps activated my faith and kept it in tact for the past fifteen years:

Step one is to understand that the situation is temporary. After receiving discouraging opinions that my daughter may never read on grade level, I convinced myself that this is based solely on how she was performing at that time. This comes under the umbrella of "a temporary situation".

The second step is to use hope to map out the ideal situation you want to see. I visualized my daughter reading and understanding what she read. Therefore, I began to buy her books and read for thirty minutes a day for five years. My expectation was that everything would turn out successfully and eventually my hopeful ideal visualization would manifest.

Believing in myself and activating my faith helped me continue to be consistent and persistent. Often times, I did not see proof of my visualization and became discouraged. This is why I wrote my "belief definition" mentioned earlier.

My daughter attended Pre-Kindergarten twice when she was aged three and four. From Pre-K to third grade, she was not reading on grade level. She was not able to retell a story nor tell me how her day went, nor ask me for what she needed. She simply pointed and used single words to get my attention.

Something magical and phenomenal finally happened when she was in the third grade. Using faith every day, I asked my daughter about her day, and eventually she could tell me what she did from the beginning to end. A sample of our daily conversation when I picked her up from school went...

Me: How was your day today?

Daughter: Fine.

Me: What did you do today?

Daughter: Color, swing, hurt.

Me: You were hurt today? What happened?

Daughter: Pushed.

Me: Who pushed you?

Daughter: Yes

This was a start, but it was not effective communication. Typically, I got clarification from her teacher and just prayed she told me everything. However, that was not happening because my daughter never communicated her point of view. She could not vocalize effectually, and it was frustrating.

When my daughter began to explain everything she did in chronological order, it was a magical day! She began with lessons the teacher discussed and then communicated how she interacted with her classmates, and ended with which students were bothering her.

That is when I pulled my car over, thanked God, opened the back seat door, kissed my daughter and praised her to the highest. After that, I ran around my car repeatedly as a happy mama!

There are strategies and habits we implemented to get to this successful point. Each day after school, we immediately completed her homework, reviewed vocabulary and math flash cards and put puzzles together. When we went shopping, I would have my daughter identify different foods in the store. Before bed, we would read for at least thirty minutes, and I would ask her to retell the story. If there was anything to cover from her speech sessions, then we worked on those as well.

The third and final step is to speak to the situation as though what you are seeking has already happened. This was so confusing at first. I needed to do this because everyone else was stating what my daughter could NOT do. I adopted another outlook with faith. I had to believe that it was taking place only 'right now'!

When my daughter brought her report card home, it contained low 'twos', and we desired to see 'fours'. I looked into her face and said, "I am so glad you are receiving 'fours' on your report card." She would say, "I hate math". I would respond, "I am so happy that you are an 'A' student in math." It did not make sense when people heard me speak like this, but it worked! My daughter went on to take Calculus her senior year in high school!

When I converse with students, I talk to them as if they are already what they desire to be. If they confide that they want to be engineers, teachers, lawyers or scientists, then I communicate to them as if they already achieved their goals. Visualize what you want. I envision students walking across the stage receiving their high school and college diplomas.

This keeps my faith sharp. I speak to students in this manner daily as I continue to do for both my daughter and son.

CHAPTER 3:

Communicate Effectively

I am a direct and candid communicator. This is not usually a welcomed approach, so I formed an empowering way to communicate with teachers, counselors, staff and students.

I realized that you do not have to be a skilled or eloquent conversationalist to achieve your desired outcome. You just need to figure out the dynamics of the system (school, nursing home, mental health, etc.) and be aware of the environment/culture to be an effective advocate, coach or mentor.

I had to find out specific contacts for particular situations. If I question whether a student is on track to graduate or not, the first person I address is the registrar who supplied me with his/her transcript. After reviewing the transcript, I am able to schedule an appointment with the guidance counselor. If you are dealing with a specific objective/goal on a student IEP, than you talk to your IEP manager first before contacting everyone else on the IEP team.

It is a tremendous help if you are an amiable person who encourages others. This is what allowed my visualized aspirations to manifest.

Additionally, you will have to participate in some tough conversations - so be prepared! In order to get to the core of an issue or concern, you need to find the root cause and the solution or your plans will hinder.

I was advocating for a student in 2008. He was a senior, and we wanted to ensure that he was on track to graduate from high school. So, I checked and double-checked with the counselor, and as far as we knew, this young man would be the first in his family to graduate from high school. The school notified him that he did not complete elective requirements necessary for graduation during spring semester of the school year. Well, just imagine how the student and I felt. Trying to find the words to explain this to his parents was challenging.

After getting this news, I met with the counselor and reminded her that she advised us with surety that all courses were completed. She was not happy with me, but I engaged in an arduous conversation in effort to get this situation solved. With diligence and dedication, the student completed the course and graduated. Sometimes difficult and uncomfortable conversations are essential in overseeing student success.

Lastly, communication is not just about talking to people face to face, and it is not simply imparting the negative aspects all of the time. Situations with my children and high school students I assist are massive undertakings, but I made sure then and now to keep a balance.

I send emails, cards and letters to teachers and counselors when I have concerns and when I want to praise them as well. One 'big hit' teachers love is when I write a letter to the building principal and assistant superintendent commending specific teachers. Each year, I continue to send updates to former teachers about my children's progress as well.

CHAPTER 4:

Team Player Mentality

D o you have Team-Player Mentality? My definition of team-player mentality is, "We all win, or we all lose." I found that there are not any true individual victories. A great example of the team-player mentality is the '4x100' relay in track. I enjoyed being on the '4x100' relay team and had so much fun running that race! It consists of four runners who not only practice together but also communicate with each other. Runners get to know each other, solidify a bond and build strong relationships. This four-person team recognizes each other's weaknesses and strengths, so when it is time they run a race to win.

During a relay race, each runner efficiently passes the baton to the next. When a runner drops the baton or does not exchange it in a timely pace, the entire team is disqualified. Teammates will pinpoint which sprinter is at fault for the failure, but the entire team is held responsible and accountable for the disqualification.

The '4x100' relay can be used as a lesson in the education arena too. Each person (teacher, counselor, principal, student, parent, after-school instructor) must run his or her race to the best of their ability. We must all do our part fully so in the end we all win!

When a team member chooses not to run their best race, we see the achievement gap widen. Bullying will prevail; absenteeism will climb; and the high school graduation and college enrollment rates will fall. After that, the overall experience for the student turns out to be non-successful.

On the other hand, when team members run their race to the best of their ability, this achievement gap closes, and bullying is no longer tolerated. Over-all attendance increases and high school graduation and college enrollment rates increase.

I never would have been able to accomplish academic success for my children and the students I serve without the assistance and efforts of remarkable people. This is why I am actually grateful for the IEP team. I get the opportunity to have the attention of the principal, counselor, social worker, teacher(s), speech therapist, psychologist, secretary and anyone who has an impact on my child's learning.

CHAPTER 5:

The IQ Factor

What is your 'I Quit' Factor? Generally, we know instantly what could cause us to quit and give up. There must be a solid commitment to unlock people's maximum potential by showing them how to go from having potential to realizing and obtaining their dreams and goals. Therefore, you need to know your IQ factor. Write down circumstances that could potentially cause you to quit and then rectify those issues and concerns.

This is what I had to do. I wrote down probable situations that could contribute to me giving up. One of my IQ factors was realizing that not every person had high expectations for my children. So it was a given that I needed to have the highest expectations instead of communicating present disheartened situations.

Therefore, when I met people with low expectations, my first thought was, "I QUIT" because being alone in the effort is never a good feeling.

I still have to encourage and remind myself that no matter what the situation looks like, I must continue the mission of advocating. Understanding children (including my own) required school for fourteen years (pre-k to 12th grade). I knew I would have to commit at least that amount of time.

By no means or in any circumstance would I allow myself to quit. I had to monitor my attitude levels at all times in order for me to stay focused and not give up. When I began to fall or develop a poor attitude, I reminded myself of the commitment I made to advocate. When my IQ Factor was high, I made sure that I did not schedule any important meetings with educators. I waited until my attitude was in tip-top condition!

CHAPTER 6:

Information Seeker

S ince I am not an actual educator, I was unaware of the curriculum and standards students must comprehend for each grade level at the time. Thus, ample questions and endless hours in the school libraries and bookstores began. Being an avid Internet surfer, I found an abundance of information online also.

I read considerable volumes of books and purchased learning software for children. Knowledge of the 'educational lingo' teachers and counselors used helped me fit in. Most importantly to me, being well informed rewarded me with the trust of these educational teams.

Personality and skill assessments such as Learning Styles Inventory, True Colors and the Five Love Languages were instrumental in the success of my relationships with my children and the students I serve. Assessments can be fun, and students enjoy finding out about themselves. It makes them feel valuable. Once we receive assessments, I teach students how to ask their teachers for ways to improve their academic grade and overall learning atmosphere at school. These assessments give me enhanced insight on how I can best serve students in strategizing a plan with the teacher.

Often I was not gaining the breakthrough expected with my daughter. We had gone two years without any progress - which was stressful. I felt that I was racing against this giant clock of success! Thus, my situation seemed enormous and overwhelming.

Complimenting her appearance worked for us. When she was five years old, I praised her on how pretty her hair ribbons were and how smart she was. The little notes in her pocket or backpack with sweet comments of encouragement were motivational as well. She loved finding them! In addition, on holidays or when teachers asked for treats, I brought the treats the teacher requested. Children enjoy their parents sharing in classroom experiences.

Providing words of affirmation to my daughter had great progress within two weeks. This was my first revelation and training on how to build a person's self-esteem and self-worth. It was phenomenal, and I had fun doing it!

CHAPTER 7:

Stick-to-it-iveness

B riefly mentioned earlier, "stick-to-it-iveness" is definitely crucial to accomplish being the best advocate, mentor and coach. Remaining consistent and persistent until you achieve the goal is always the plan.

Being patient until you see the visualized desire can often become daunting and discouraging. Nevertheless, I remember my mom saying to me, "The race is not given to the swift or to the strong but to him/her who endures until the end." Endurance is what makes us win in this life.

When I think of 'stick-to-it-iveness', I picture dandelions in my mom's yard. It is extremely difficult to get rid of them. Just when I thought I sprayed enough "dandelion eradication solution", they reappeared. This resulted in me cutting my mom's grass weekly.

When the dandelions would come back up, I knew it was time to cut the grass again! You must be as persistent and sometimes as annoying as dandelions. A commitment to ensuring that the people you serve get a fair chance is a task, and you will may not be favored often. You must stick to what you are doing, and you will get the desired results.

CHAPTER 8:

The Art of Asking Questions

Asking questions that produce constructive results is an art. They nature of questions should be open-ended to gain a true understanding of what someone is trying to communicate to you.

I have concluded that you need to do three things be a master of this art form: ask investigative questions only, repeat the answer for clarification and knowledge of the situation and ascertain the best way to move forward.

During my first few IEP meetings, I did not understand the educators' language so had to ask a great deal of questions. In the beginning, the questions I asked did not assist me in making the essential decisions regarding my children because I did not have a clear understanding of what I heard from them.

Although I could tell people were getting irritated from my inquiries, I persisted. I could only continue to advocate with clarity. Now, I am completely comfortable asking questions.

These four types of questions work well:

Goal Questions - What are the challenges the student is struggling with at this moment? What new skills do you want the student to learn or develop?

Reality Questions - What is working well and not so well for the student? What has the student done so far to improve?

Option Questions - What is the most helpful element we can do now? If you were guaranteed 'success', what would you do?

Way Forward Questions - How are we going to celebrate when we reach our goal? On a scale of 1 to 10, how motivated are you in attaining this goal?

CHAPTER 9:

Call to Action

Thank you for going on this quick and scripted journey with me. I gained considerably too by writing about my experience. I cannot be silent when I know there are parents and students out there who are not aware that they can win academically, personally and socially.

Imagine what would have happened if I had given up when my daughter was three years old. I definitely would not have had the opportunity to be an empowered advocate for my daughter, son or the students whom I work with and serve now.

This experience has shown me that people give up on students too early. This can be overwhelming for their parents. This included me as a working parent who worked long hours. Coming home after seven pm most nights and working with my children until midnight was not easy. It has been worth it though. The most important piece

I have learned through this process is to keep the student's success in the forefront of our minds. This will never lead us wrong as we advocate for them. I am thankful to have worked along-side phenomenal teachers, principals and educators. This powerful team allowed me to accomplish such success.

Is there anyone in your community who needs you? Are you troubled by what you see or hear regarding certain life subjects or situations? Have you overcome a life issue and can show others how to turn into 'over comers'? You can do something significant.

Go out and conduct simple acts of kindness, guide people to success or anything else. Someone needs you! There are students, parents, school systems, the elderly and more people whom you can affect in a positive way. You can change lives!

Are you willing to be the change you want to see? This is my call to action for you. Be the change you want to realize in your family, in your community, and most importantly your life.

The outcomes of an inspired advocate have and will continue to be a rewarding experience for me. Now I hope these attributes will prove to be rewarding for you as well.

Remember the eight attributes every advocate must embrace:

- Believe in Yourself

- Have Faith

- Communicate Effectively

- Know Your IQ Factor

- Always have the Team-Player Mentality

- Be an Information Seeker

- Stick-to-it-iveness is a Must

- Master the Art of Asking Questions

Now......go out and be an Advocate Who Inspires!

Bio

R honda grew up in Wichita, KS with humble beginnings and in a loving household primarily raised by her mother. She visited her father annually up to the year he committed suicide when she was in tenth grade. Growing up on welfare, government cash assistance and food stamps powered Rhonda to have grit.

She graduated high school without getting the best grades yet had a warm heart and a friendly personality. Rhonda earned a Bachelor's Degree in Marketing from Wichita State University and her Master's in Management Information Systems from Friends University. She has two children who are both attending college. Rhonda enjoys reading, encouraging people, watching super hero movies, having fun and advocating.

Rhonda credits her mother, Hazel Thomas, for instilling in her the unwavering value of a good education. Emalyn Rogers, Rhonda's high school counselor, the TRIO Talent Search and TRIO Student Support Services Program, worked diligently to ensure that she obtained a college degree.

There are hosts of people who have supported and encouraged Rhonda along her awesome journey. Now she pays it forward on a daily basis.

A quote by Dr. Martin Luther King Jr. is the catalyst that keeps Rhonda advocating, "*Our lives begin to end the day we become silent about things that matter*". Education Matters.

CPSIA information can be obtained
at www.ICGtesting.com
Printed in the USA
BVHW062309140820
586425BV00004B/229